PSD2
in Plain Eng

CW00847991

Rohan Consulting Services Limited
Level 1, The Chase,
Carmanhall Road,
Sandyford,
Dublin,
Ireland
D18 Y3X2

paulrohan@rohanconsult.com

ISBN-978-1517598556

All design, development, layout, proofs and
infographics by Ellen Egan at eganellen.com

Contents

About the Author

Paul Rohan is a researcher and management consultant in payment systems and payments regulations. Paul advises Payment Institutions and other service providers in the EU Payments and Fintech markets. He also consults on business strategy with traditional banks. Paul has a specific focus on helping clients make a successful transition into the era of Open Banking APIs.

Paul received undergraduate degrees in Business from University College Dublin and Financial Information Systems from Trinity College Dublin. Paul holds an MSc in Programme Management from UCD Michael Smurfit Graduate Business School. Paul brings decades of experience as a leading industry practitioner to his advisory clients.

Acknowledgements

Thank you to Robert O'Neill, David Ivor Smith and Damian Allen for their input and advice. I am very grateful to Ellen Egan, my graphic designer.

Love to Belinda, David, Anna and Stephen.

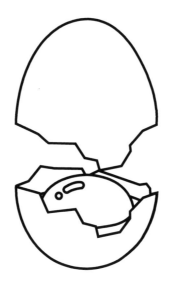

PSD2
in Plain English

Introduction

EU law makers want more competition and innovation in payments. They are unhappy that payment services from banks are very similar.

There are some logical reasons why payment services can be similar.

Customers want their payments to travel smoothly between all banks. Banks need common standards on the data in payments and the timing of payments. One bank cannot set standards on its own. This causes the features of a payment service to be similar across banks. This can reduce the product features that are different and this reduces innovation.

Payment accounts do a lot of useful things for customers. They are the gateway to cash services, card services, electronic transfers and direct debits. Online banking offers convenient ways for customers to place deposits and request loans. Many customers are slow to change this convenient service.

Banks can serve many millions of customers that make hundreds of millions of payments. Banks have the benefits of very large scale and can add more customers with only a small increase in costs. A payment account is not a very expensive service. Mobile phones, household energy, insurance, refuse collection and many other routine services are usually more expensive. This reduces the number of customers that shop around for payment services.

Established banks focus mostly on their existing customers. They have successful products and they try to improve those products. Innovating is not easy. It can be difficult to judge the pace of change because technology can improve faster than the demand for that technology.

It is not easy for a bank to pull staff away from established methods. Shareholders in banks expect profits to grow solidly. Established banks worry about making poor investments in new technology. They worry that new technology won't be used by their existing customers.

Established banks listen to their customers but customers aren't trained to assess new financial technology. Banks have lots of knowledge about the products that have made them successful. It is not easy to break the mould.

EU law makers are trying to break the mould with PSD2. It points banks towards new business models. PSD2 has a defined timetable and banks must organise project teams to examine PSD2. They must pull key staff away from established methods and they must engage in new and innovative methods.

PSD2 introduces a new legal structure to payments in the EU. It could cause a strong ripple effect that could change the entire financial services market.

This book explains PSD2 to business professionals who are not payments experts. It shows how payments data could be a key ingredient in new service innovations. It explains how the business models of traditional banks could change.

New Digital Economy

APIs

There is a new law that introduces APIs into EU banking. It is a Payment Services Directive. As it is the EU's second Payment Services Directive, it is known as "PSD2".

Computer programs are often designed with a person in mind. However, the output from a program can also be used by another computer program. This type of program doesn't try to offer a pleasing experience for a person. These are called APIs and API is short for Application Programming Interface. An API offers data and tasks designed to be used by software. An API is "machine-readable" rather than "human-readable". There are three types of APIs: private, partner and public.

A Private API is used internally to integrate different systems used by a firm. They help streamline systems and they reduce the costs of change. Private APIs increase flexibility and improve day-to-day operations.

A Partner API helps integrate software between a firm and a business partner. There are commercial contracts that are drawn up for the Partner API. They add value to a relationship between two firms and they help two firms do lots of business together. Some business partners insist on APIs to handle the flow of activities. Partner APIs can be a stepping stone for companies to offer Public APIs.

A Public API is published like a website. Public APIs allow firms to publicly reveal functions and data from their systems. Other firms can then use these Public APIs. The firms that use the Public APIs don't necessarily have a wider relationship with the API Provider.

A firm with good Public APIs can attract a community of API Developers. They design products that are powered by the Public APIs. A community of API Developers can help improve the products of a firm and the firm can reach new markets. They help increase business activity and new ways of making profits can be found.

Although they are both published, a Public API is quite different from a website. Companies must learn new skills to publish APIs. Publishing websites is quite straightforward. A firm puts material on its website and people use the website. People don't have to sign a contract to use the website. If the website changes, the next visitors see the new materials. The browsers that people use are not affected by any changes to the materials.

If a firm changes its website, people see the material changed or laid out differently. People can quickly adjust and find what they need. With APIs it's different. Unlike people, computer programs are built on top of APIs and can't adjust to changes. So, companies try not to change APIs unexpectedly as this would cause serious knock-on effects.

The design of an API has to be documented accurately. The API provider describes what the API does and says when the API is available. The API provider may limit the times that a computer program can use the API. The API provider may set legal limits on how the API is used and API users have to agree to follow the rules.

APIs are like things in the real world. **An API can be compared to an electricity wall socket.** A wall socket is an interface to an electricity service. In practical terms, people don't use an electricity service. People use devices that in turn use an electricity service.

Wall sockets have predictable patterns of openings. Electrical plugs match predictable patterns of openings in the wall sockets. The electricity coming into the socket also has specifications, such as voltage.

The designers of TVs know what to expect of wall sockets and wall sockets are designed to know what to expect from TVs. In a similar way, an API sets out how two pieces of software should work together.

APIs are a great help to service suppliers. They are an "endpoint". An endpoint is the final stage of a process. A wall socket is an endpoint with a standard interface and an electricity supplier can make changes behind this endpoint. The source of power can be switched from a coal-burning plant to a wind farm. The wires on the street can be changed from above ground to underground. The systems that monitor the electric grid can be changed. The same principle holds true for APIs. Any changes behind the API endpoint are not noticed by the software that uses the API.

APIs also help service users, in the same way that users benefit from wall sockets. Users don't have to physically connect their TVs to electric wiring in the walls of buildings. Moving a TV from one room to another is easy. TV designers don't worry about the wiring in the walls and they don't worry about any other devices that use the same wiring. TV designers don't worry about how or where the electricity is generated. This allows designers to focus on developing good TVs.

A piece of software can plug into an API endpoint to get data. It can also plug into an API endpoint to do automated tasks. A Smartphone App for home buyers can offer an interactive map by plugging into Google Maps. Each time that App displays a new map, it uses a Public API published by Google.

Google might charge a fee for using the mapping API. A developer can decide to pay to use an API or to develop a similar program. The developer can also look for a cheaper provider of a similar API. APIs make the economy more efficient.

APIs help software developers because fetching certain data can be tricky. Designing certain automated tasks can be complex and these complex activities can happen quite often. APIs can turn this into a few lines of computer code that can be repeated many times. Programmers don't have to "reinvent the wheel" in every new program. They can focus on the unique parts of their software.

A business accepting credit card payments is a good example of the value of APIs. It's a waste of time if developers working on an App to hail taxis also have to build credit card acceptance software. It is faster to use a specialist API provider.

In some areas, there are many API providers competing to be the most useful API. Credit card acceptance, mapping, navigation and language translation are all very competitive areas. Many API providers compete for the attention of developers. We are moving towards a world where lots of software will use APIs bought "off-the-shelf".

APIs are available through the Internet and they offer many opportunities for innovation.

Some of the innovations are aimed at consumers. Taxi services call a credit card acceptance API from across the Internet. Thousands of developers have software that uses mapping APIs. People use APIs offered by social media platforms to broadcast photos from photo-sharing Apps.

The API Economy has many possibilities because APIs change the way that software can be delivered. Many firms are changing business strategies in order to use APIs. There are thousands of firms now providing APIs and these firms are from hundreds of industries.

The API Economy has flexible ways of sharing data. Sometimes the Developer pays for using an API or pays for different types of access through an API. Developers could pay under a usage-based scheme or pay for the amount of data they get.

Some APIs are made available to API Developers free of charge. This happens when an API Provider wants to spread their data and programs throughout the market.

Sometimes the API Developer gets paid by the API Provider to help drive traffic to the Provider's website. Sometimes an API Developer is rewarded for a specific result, if the Developer helps refer business or new sales to a Provider. These rewards can be once-off or they can be repeated.

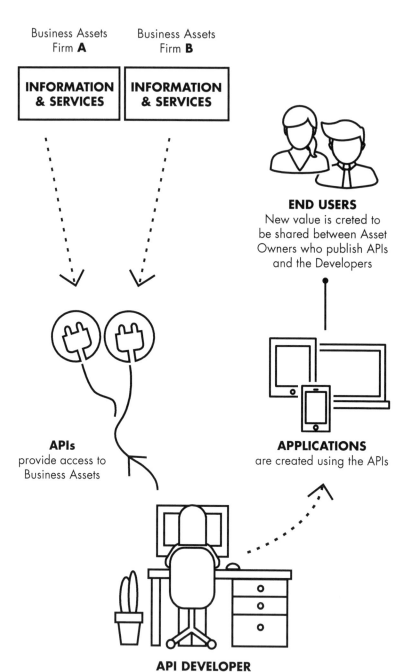

Business Assets
Firm **A**

Business Assets
Firm **B**

INFORMATION & SERVICES

INFORMATION & SERVICES

END USERS
New value is creted to be shared between Asset Owners who publish APIs and the Developers

APIs
provide access to Business Assets

APPLICATIONS
are created using the APIs

API DEVELOPER
Puts the APIs to work to create applications

New Rules and New Players

PSD2

PSD2 is introducing new methods that are unique in world banking. PSD2 will allow firms to electronically instruct a bank to make a payment from a customer's payment account. The firm needs the customer's permission to make the payment.

PSD2 will also allow a firm to take data from a payment account to help offer a service. A customer will have to agree to the data being shared and the data can only be used to provide the agreed service.

These firms will need permission from EU regulators to offer these services. The only practical way for banks to comply with PSD2 is to build APIs. APIs will allow banks to securely open functions and data from their systems.

Regulated firms will not need a commercial contract with banks to use the PSD2 APIs. PSD2 does not mean that a payments service is free. A customer might pay 5 cents to make a payment from their account at a bank. The same customer can ask a regulated provider to use the bank's PSD2 APIs to make a payment. The customer still pays the bank a fee of 5 cents.

PSD2 APIs must be made available to API Developers free of charge. All banks in the EU will join the API economy because of PSD2.

EU law makers did not design PSD2 just to encourage the use of APIs. EU law makers had many reasons to introduce PSD2. They want to prompt more competition. Many EU banks were supported by Governments during the 2008 financial crisis and the reputations of those banks suffered greatly. They still have the same market share despite this damage to their brands. This showed EU law makers that more competition is needed.

PSD2 will bring new competition as providers will design new services that use PSD2 APIs. They will build new relationships with bank customers. PSD2 APIs will help introduce new providers of routine financial services. There will be more providers with small market shares and EU regulators will find it easier to let a struggling provider go out of business.

EU law makers are also concerned about SMEs having access to loans. SMEs can find it difficult to get loans from banks and this is a big issue for EU law makers. An individual SME doesn't employ many people. However, there are many SMEs in the EU and SMEs are big employers overall. Many SMEs rely heavily on bank loans to expand their businesses. The payments in bank accounts tell a lot about the health of a business. New lenders won't have to manage an SME's payment account to get this valuable information. The PSD2 APIs will allow new lenders to get more data so they will compete more effectively.

EU law makers would also like to see EU businesses becoming more competitive in digital services. The global markets in digital services are very competitive and they are very valuable. Very few digital EU businesses are becoming successful across the world. The US and China are far more likely to grow these businesses. EU law makers would like to break down barriers within the single EU digital market. This will help growing EU businesses get more customers within the EU. This success would help these businesses to grow to a global size.

PSD1 became law in EU Member States in 2009 and it built a legal framework for payment services in the EU. The main innovation in PSD1 was to create a new legal type of payments service provider. These were named "Payment Institutions". Payment Institutions are not allowed take deposits from the public. They can only control customers' money while they are making payments.

EU law makers had a review of PSD1 in 2012 that gathered a lot of information. The EU law makers spoke to providers of payment services and they consulted local regulators in Member States. A survey of payments users was carried out. The review consulted consumer associations across the EU.

The EU law makers wanted to see if there had been any problems with PSD1. They wanted to see if PSD1 had reduced payments prices and helped develop more modern services.

The reviewers decided that PSD1 had reached some of its aims. PSD1 had streamlined the speed of payments and payments were moving faster. The features of payments were now easier to understand and there was a lot more legal consistency. Payments users had few complaints about the new PSD1 standards.

PSD1 rules made sure that Payment Institutions were prudent. Payment Institutions had to have capital when they were set up and they had to have their own money in reserve at all times. They had to make sure that customers' money didn't get mixed up with their money. The 2012 review showed that Payment Institutions had followed the PSD1 rules.

The review thought that some other PSD1 aims were not achieved. Very few new providers emerged to enter the payments market. The cost of payment services for the payments users didn't fall significantly. Payments were moving faster but there had been few new innovations.

The review showed that only 32% of providers had expanded their services into other EU states. When providers did expand, they only moved into 3 or 4 of the 28 Member States.

Payments Institutions needed banks to help them offer their services. The PSD1 review found that banks could be unwilling to open bank accounts for Payment Institutions.

Some people were unhappy that PSD1 only covered payments that moved within the EU. Payments to family outside the EU by immigrants and migrant workers were not protected by PSD1.

Account Servicing PSPs, PISPs and AISPs

PSD1 did not achieve the innovation and competition wanted by EU law makers. PSD2 has set up new legal structures to provide that innovation and competition.

The innovative new providers are legally called "Payment Initiation Service Providers (PISPs)" and "Account information Service Providers (AISPs)".

PISPs and AISPs need permission from Regulators to take on these roles.

PSD2 sets out how PISPs and AISPs have to interact with "Account Servicing Payment Service Providers (AS PSPs)". Account Servicing PSP is a new legal term to describe payments service providers that offer payments accounts. In practical terms, Account Servicing PSPs are the banks that offer payment accounts.

New Types of Payment Service Provider within PSD2	Account Servicing Payment Service Provider	Payment Initiation Service Provider	Account Information Service Provider
Short Form	AS PSP	PISP	AISP
Other Legal Roles	Credit Institution	Payment Institution	Payment Institution
PSD2 Role	A Payment Service Provider (PSP) providing and maintaining payment accounts for a payer.	A Payment Service Provider (PSP) offering a payment initiation service. This is a service to initiate a payment from a payment account at the request of the user. The account is held at another PSP.	A Payment Service Provider (PSP) offering an account information service. This is an online service to provide consolidated information on one or more payment accounts held at one or more PSPs.

PSD2 became EU Law in January 2016. EU law makers asked the European Banking Authority (EBA) to help implement the new law. The EBA is an independent authority and its job is to maintain financial stability. The EBA watches for new risks in the EU banking sector. **The EBA develops a Single Rulebook for financial services and the guidelines and standards for PSD2 will be part of the Single Rulebook.**

The EBA will set guidelines on the information needed when a provider applies to be a PISP or AISP. They have to explain their business plans and they need evidence of financial reserves. Applicants will have to show how they will handle security and privacy. The EBA sets the amount of professional insurance that PISPs and AISPs need and the amount of insurance will depend on their ambitions. The EBA will take into account if the PISP or AISP has just payment services or has other businesses. The EBA will set guidelines on the security measures to be taken.

Guidelines will be set for Regulators to share information on security threats. The EBA will publish a central register of PISPs and AISPs. There will be guidelines for managing security incidents and how to handle complaints. There will be complaints if PSD2 rules are not being followed. EBA guidelines come into effect as soon as they are published.

The EBA will set Technical Standards for PSD2. This is more complex than setting guidelines. The standards cannot force providers to use particular types of technology. The Technical Standards will have to be precise and everyone must understand them in the same way. The Technical Standards will show how to conduct PSD2 business but they cannot be so rigid that they stop new innovations.

The Technical Standards will safeguard security details and set out how providers and customers will communicate. Electronic communications must follow common Technical Standards.

Technical Standards will explain how to identify a major security incident. There will be rules on who to notify if that happens.

The most important Technical Standard is for "strong customer authentication". Providers must have robust ways of identifying users and other service providers. PSD2 defines strong customer authentication as needing "two or more elements". These two elements will come from three things. The first thing is something only the user knows (knowledge). The second thing is something only the user has (a possession). The third thing is something the user is (something in-built).

These two or more things must be separate from each other. If a thief captures one, the other thing must still be safe. They need to keep the users' data fully secure. In recent times, strong authentication typically meant passwords and PIN numbers. In future, biometrics and other new techniques could be used too.

Setting Technical Standards is a big challenge. Many new payments standards have been set in the EU in recent years, such as SEPA. The SEPA standards development process was a harmonising challenge and it was not new and radical. There were "best of breed" payments standards in Member States to show the way. The participants in the SEPA process were mostly banks and the general designs of existing schemes were understood by many people.

Both banks and other providers will take part in the PSD2 standards development. PISPs and AISPs are new legal entities. New business models could emerge that are not anticipated and setting Technical Standards is not straightforward.

The EBA will consult all the providers as they develop Technical Standards and they will listen very carefully to new providers. The proposed Technical Standards are delivered by the EBA to the European Commission. The European Commission has to accept them and the EU Council and the European Parliament are also consulted.

EU law makers want more competition and they will remove barriers to innovative new services. **They don't want new competitors to face too much "red tape".** This would slow down their entry into the market.

There are different levels of "red tape" for new providers. PSD2 sets a low barrier to entry for AISPs. New providers will face less red tape if they want to be AISPs only. AISPs have to explain their proposed services. They have to use bank data as agreed with the customer. They have to have a business plan and they need proof of suitable systems and resources. Regulators will pay attention to security and data protection.

An AISP must have professional insurance based on the amount of data taken from Account Servicing PSPs. A provider acting just as an AISP will not initiate payments. PSD2 does not require them to hold capital. Firms acting just as AISPs can gain access to data without money laundering controls.

Banks acting as Account Servicing PSPs initiate payments for the user and are in control of the money. PISPs also initiate payments for users but do not take control of the money. The PSD2 rules take this into account. Unlike Account Servicing PSPs, PISPs don't have to have a very large amount of their own capital.

PSD2 does have minimum requirements for PISPs and AISPs. There are strict rules about outsourcing. PISPs and AISPs will have to report to regulators. They must explain their services clearly to users and the fees that they charge must be easy for users to understand.

Banks acting as Account Servicing PSPs must treat PISPs and AISP fairly. Banks cannot force PISPs and AISPs to sign a commercial agreement or force PISPs and AISPs to carry out their business in a particular way. Banks cannot treat PISPs or AISPs as a low priority or put payments initiated by PISPs at the end of the queue.

There could be evidence of fraud or unauthorised access to an account. In that case, banks can refuse to take instructions from a PISP or AISP. PSD2 says that banks must give reasons if they refuse.

New Ingredient: Payment Account Data

Cardless Shopping

The review of PSD1 found some useful innovations. "Payment initiation services" had begun outside PSD1 rules. A user asks a payments service provider to access a payment account to initiate a payment. The payment initiation service that accesses the account is not the service that operates the account.

Shops don't like paying the fees charged to accept payment cards. Visa and Mastercard are the two biggest card schemes. Cards are usually given to shoppers by the bank that operates their payment accounts. These cards are designed by card schemes.

Shops use a provider that handles or "acquires" card payments. It can be through a device on a shop counter. It can be through a checkout button on a website. If users are shopping online, they input their card details. The acquiring card firm contacts the card scheme. The card scheme takes the payment from the shopper's payment account or adds it to their credit card bill.

Payment initiation services are offering shops another way of taking online payments. This will bring new competition for Visa and Mastercard. The payment initiation service provider lets the shopper pay directly from their payment account.

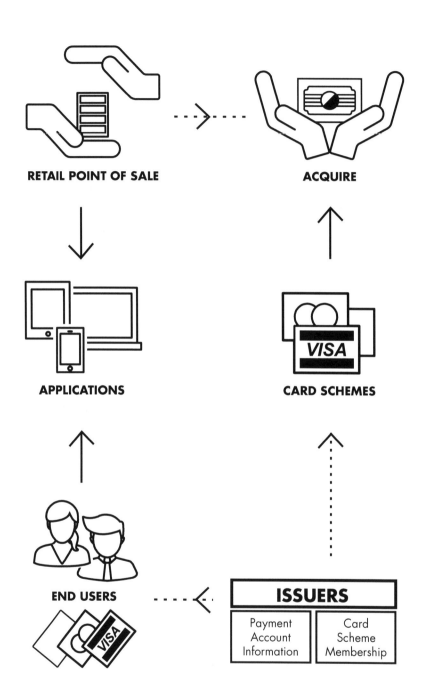

RETAIL POINT OF SALE

ACQUIRE

APPLICATIONS

CARD SCHEMES

END USERS

ISSUERS	
Payment Account Information	Card Scheme Membership

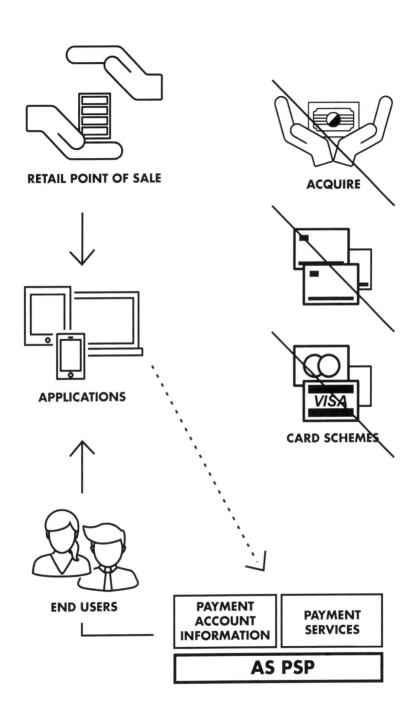

RETAIL POINT OF SALE

ACQUIRE

APPLICATIONS

CARD SCHEMES

END USERS

PAYMENT ACCOUNT INFORMATION	PAYMENT SERVICES
AS PSP	

To use the service, the buyer selects a product on a website. They then select the bank that operates their payment account. The payment initiation service automatically directs the customer to their online banking website. The price of the product and the shop's account details are loaded into the online banking website. The shopper inputs the correct security details for the online banking service. The payment goes from the shopper's account to the shop's account and the card schemes are not involved.

This is a valuable innovation because users can shop online without a credit or debit card. The payment initiation service shows that the shopper has approved the payment and that they can't change their mind. This allows the shop to ship the product immediately.

EU law makers were pleased to see this new innovation because it is new competition for the card schemes. However, they had concerns that these new services weren't covered by PSD1. Things could go wrong and there were no arrangements for managing disputes. There was no formal contract between the service provider and the bank. The shopper was also providing their security details to the service and it was not fully clear if that disclosure was legal.

Shops are very pleased with the new competition for the card schemes. The card schemes have a very strong position in the market. Cards are very popular with payments users because they have been around a long time. The first Credit Card system began in California in 1958 and it later became the VISA scheme.

Card schemes have balancing fees called Interchange. These fees are paid by the firms that manage cards for shops. These fees are paid to the banks that issue cards to shoppers. Interchange fees are designed to share out rewards from card use and to encourage card firms and banks to cooperate. If they cooperate, the use of cards grows.

Cards have become very popular and they are accepted almost everywhere. Billions of cards have been issued since 1958. It is difficult for new payments innovations to compete with the card schemes.

EU law makers believe that the costs of accepting card payments are too high. Card firms serving shops charge fees that are higher than Interchange. EU law makers believe that high Interchange fees give card schemes an unfair advantage. They have set a limit on the level of Interchange Fees and they hope that this will reduce the fees paid by shops to accept cards.

The limit on Interchange has made cards a less profitable service for banks. Banks can see that shops are using payment initiation services and that shoppers like the option of paying from their payment account. Bank customers that don't want cards can now shop online.

There had been concerns in banks that the new payment initiation services weren't covered by PSD1. PSD2 is bringing new legal certainty to these services. PSD2 has new arrangements for managing disputes. The customer can use a payment initiation service in an official and regulated way.

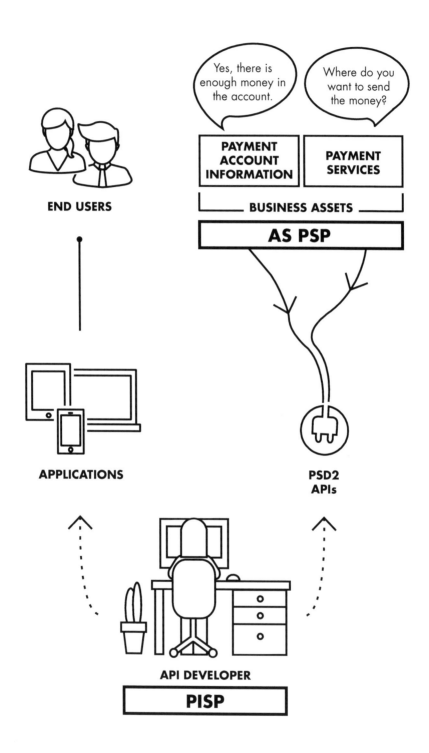

A PISP will receive information from the payer's Account Servicing PSP on the availability of funds through PSD2 APIs. The Account Servicing PSP will give the PISP a "yes/no answer". The answer will be "Yes" if the payer has enough money for the payment to proceed. The Account Servicing PSP doesn't tell the PISP anything else. The Account Servicing PSP could know that the payer has millions of euro in the payment account. The PISP will only know that the payer can make a 100-euro payment from the account. The payment can only proceed if the payer gives an explicit approval. The payer must give approval each time that his chosen PISP initiates a payment.

PSD2 will offer online shoppers a choice between card payments and payments made directly from their payment accounts. Shops could encourage competition by offering loyalty points or other benefits. Shoppers could get loyalty points if they choose the cheapest payment method for the shop.

Personal Finances

There were new innovations outside PSD1 to gather data from payment accounts. "Account information services (AIS)" helped users to gather information from payment accounts held with different banks. This can give users an overall view of their finances at a given time.

The AIS connected directly to the online service of the user's bank using the security details issued by the bank. The most common type of AIS is a Personal Financial Management service.

Personal Financial Management (PFM) is a set of digital tools. They tell a consumer if they are spending more than they are saving. A PFM tool gathers information from various accounts that show spending. A payment account or a credit card account shows the shop or the seller beside each payment. PFM tools automatically sort the shops and sellers into different types of spending.

The banking industry has never set a standard method to provide account data to these PFM providers. PFM providers have been using a method called "screen scraping" to get the data. This method is decades old. Moving data between computer programs should be a very structured process. It needs to be structured because there are no people involved. The documentation of the process has to be very detailed and there needs to be absolute certainty in the arrangements.

A screen scrape is a crude method of gathering data. It takes the output from a computer program that was designed to be viewed by a human. The output is not designed to be input for another computer program.

It is neither documented nor clearly broken up into logical steps. A computer programmer can "screen scrape" output to use as an input. A screen scrape scans the program output that creates a screen for a person to look at. The screen scape ignores the parts that arranges and labels the screen. It reads the output like a map, looking for numbers and text.

A screen scrape is a "last resort" when there is no other way to get data for a computer program. They are hard to design because displays intended for people on websites can change often. People can cope with this easily but a computer program gets confused when this happens. Screen scraping is a crude and old way of getting data and the process breaks easily. The activity can cause spikes in volume to online banking websites and the activity can look like a hacking attack. Banks often have to keep a "safe list" of screen scrapers that they will allow scrape out the customer data.

Some banks track where the scraping is coming from and they restrict the screen scraping to certain times of the day. If bank systems are overloaded or unstable, banks stop the screen scraping. Consumers who only use the online banking service are pushed to the top of the queue.

Consumers often don't know who to call if the scraping fails. The consumer may call the PFM provider when a link to an account is broken or the provider might tell a consumer to call the bank. The PFM provider may not have spotted a change to a bank's website.

Screen scraping is less secure than modern methods of getting data. Users handing over their online banking user names and passwords to PFM providers is far from ideal. PFM start-ups may not make security a high priority. In some countries, Regulators have instructed that screen scraping of bank data be stopped. Thefts from payment accounts and thefts of identities do happen. It happens when users lose control of their User ID and Password.

Payment service providers can add extra layers of security. They can send a text message to the user's phone. Extra security layers can cause problems with crude and brittle screen scraping. Users need a replacement for screen scraping.

PFM providers are likely to become AISPs in order to use the PSD2 APIs. The PSD2 APIs will resolve the problems with screen-scraping of payment account data.

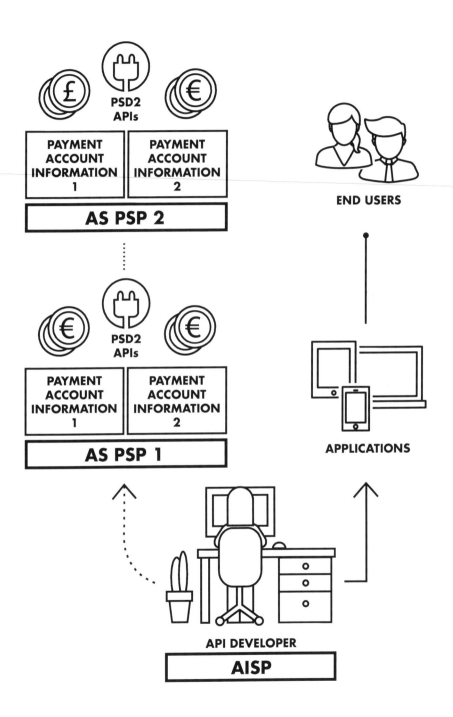

Comparing Prices

There could be demand from price comparison websites to use the PSD2 APIs. Price comparison websites help consumers save money by letting consumers compare products simply and quickly. Consumers don't pay a fee for this service because suppliers pay the websites if their product is chosen.

The websites let consumers search for deals from a wide range of products. They aim to explain how different products work. Consumers choose the ones that suit them best.

Consumers have to give time and effort to using price comparison websites. They need to know the cost of the products they already use and they need to know how they paid for the products. They could have paid by cash, cheque, card, electronic transfer or direct debit. The time and effort can reduce the benefit of price comparison websites.

Consumers often focus on their payments for regular services. Payments made for services like Cable TV, Life Assurance and Insurance can be seen in payment accounts. Utilities like energy, water and refuse collection can be paid by direct debit. These types of costs can be a big share of a household's costs.

PSD2 can reduce the effort to use price comparison websites. Payment accounts contain data on what consumers are actually spending. Under PSD2, price comparison websites can become AISPs. PSD2 could increase the use of price comparison websites.

Traditional Loans

Payments accounts hold a huge amount of general knowledge about the customers that use them.
This is true for both consumers and businesses.

The provider of an account can see a consumer's wages. Banks as Account Servicing PSPs can see the money in an account after bills are paid. Bills can be paid in a planned fashion with direct debits or they can be paid in less structured ways. The Account Servicing PSP can tell how long a consumer has lived at their address. Payments in the account can show the consumer's loans, savings and investments.

Some consumers are very organised and they always stay within the agreed terms of their account. Bills are paid on time and the consumer never makes an urgent request for credit. Account Servicing PSPs are in a good position to know the organised consumers.

A payment account also holds a lot of general knowledge about a business. The revenues coming into the business are visible and so are the profits made after suppliers are paid. The payroll payments show how many people are employed in a business and shows how much they are paid. The customers that pay electronically can be analysed. International payments in the payment account show exports, imports or both.

Some businesses are very organised and they always stay within the agreed terms of their payment account. There are never any urgent requests for credit. Banks acting as Account Servicing PSPs are in a good position to spot healthy businesses.

Bank A and Bank B might want to compete to offer a loan to a customer of Bank A. As Bank A is the Account Servicing PSP, it currently has more general knowledge about the customer than Bank B. Both banks are PSPs. They can act as PISPs and AISPs.

Acting as an AISP, Bank B can use Bank A's PSD2 APIs to access the payment account data. The customer of Bank A must give permission. The general knowledge about the customer will be available to both banks. **After PSD2, it will be less of an advantage to be the Account Servicing PSP.** Customers will benefit from the increased competition.

Peer-to-Peer Loans

New peer-to-peer lending platforms match savers and borrowers directly. Borrowers request loans on peer-to-peer websites and these platforms are becoming popular. New Peer-to-Peer platforms are quite different to banks. Peer-to-peer platforms could use payment account data from PSD2 APIs.

Banks have traditionally been "middle men" as they help the flow between deposits and loans. Savings are deposited into banks and banks then channel this money into loans. Loans help businesses and households to grow. **A depositor can provide money for many borrowers but depositors never know who the borrowers are.**

The loan contracts sit on the asset side of a bank's balance sheet and the deposit contracts sit on the liabilities side of a bank's balance sheet. Customer deposits are the lifeblood of a bank. Banks have a license to be Credit Institution and they can take deposits from the public. The law prevents Payment Institutions from taking deposits from the public.

Banks have money that they hold in reserve. It is money owned by their shareholders and this reserve of shareholders' money acts as a shock absorber. An economy can go into recession and businesses and households can struggle to repay loans on schedule. The shock absorber is used if a bank makes losses on loans. If banks are making losses, depositors still have their money returned on time.

A peer-to-peer lending platform doesn't have a balance sheet. It organises a market place where individual borrowers and individual lenders deal directly with each other. A borrower could have a problem with a loan repayment timetable and the individual lender that gave the loan suffers directly.

If an individual borrower keeps to an agreed repayment reschedule, the individual lender cannot demand their money back. This is different to a depositor in a bank because savers can get their money quickly from a bank. This is a big difference between banks and new peer-to-peer lending platforms.

Peer-to-peer lending platforms help individual borrowers and lenders find each other. Individual lenders want good information on the risks of individual borrowers so some peer-to-peer lending platforms have begun to offer risk analysis to the lenders. The platforms are trying to guide the individual lenders.

The peer-to-peer lending platforms could become AISPs under PSD2. This would help lenders have the best possible information about borrowers.

The individual borrower could be a business. There is lots of general knowledge about the business in the payment account. A lender who sees data from a payment account is in a good position to give loans. PSD2 could help the peer-to-peer lending platforms to guide lenders to borrowers that match their appetite for risk. The account data can be taken without a commercial contract with the Account Servicing PSP. PSD2 could increase the growth of peer-to-peer lending platforms in the EU.

Peer-to-Peer FX

Peer-to-peer foreign exchange (FX) platforms are growing. It is a crowdsourcing model for exchanging currency. It removes the "middle man" from currency conversion. These platforms charge a commission rate and they are undercutting banks in some market segments. They are less expensive than banks at some transaction sizes.

PSD2 allows Payment Institutions to offer some services related to payments and FX is one of those services. Payment Institutions will examine PSD2 closely to find new opportunities in FX and they will carefully examine the impact of PSD2 on currency payment accounts. Currency payment accounts are offered by Account Servicing PSPs.

Most of the currency payment accounts in the EU are offered by banks. Businesses are more active traders in foreign exchange than consumers. A currency account helps a trading business as it limits the risk and expense of changing money into home currency.

EU banks make currency accounts available in all major currencies and customers manage these accounts through online banking services. Banks can also make overdraft facilities available in different currencies. Businesses use these accounts far more actively than consumers.

A currency account can have a small number of payment types. A currency account doesn't allow currency cash to be lodged or withdrawn and they don't tend to offer direct debits. Currency accounts don't offer payment cards. A currency account usually allows electronic credit transfers. A payment account is defined by PSD2 as an account that is used for the execution of payment transactions. The credit transfers from the currency accounts mean that these accounts are covered by PSD2.

Businesses use credit transfers to pay their suppliers in other currency zones. Some businesses can demand to always be paid in their home currency but many businesses that trade in different currencies need a currency account.

19 countries of the 28 EU Member States use the euro as their currency. Lots of businesses in these countries use non-euro currency accounts for import and export activities. Some of these accounts are for trade outside the EU and some are for trade with EU Member States that don't use the euro.

9 Member States of the EU continue to use their own national currencies. Both the UK and Denmark joined the EU in 1973. They still have an opt-out from the single currency. The polls in Sweden have shown a strong "No" to eurozone membership for some time. Some of the countries who joined the EU in 2004 have no target date to adopt the euro. Romania has a target of 2019. Bulgaria and Croatia have no target date for euro adoption. Businesses in these countries hold euro currency accounts.

PSD2 covers payments in all official EU currencies. PSD2 covers payments within the European Economic Area (EEA). The EEA includes EU countries and Iceland, Liechtenstein and Norway. The EEA allows these countries to be part of the EU's single market.

The EEA is not a minor part of PSD2. Norway is one of the richest countries in the world due to its oil reserves. Norway's trade is dominated by the EU and there are many businesses inside the EU holding Norwegian Krone in currency accounts.

PSD1 applied only to payments where both providers were in the EEA. PSD2 applies to payments when one of the providers is outside the EEA. These are 'one leg-out' payments.

An AISP registered under PSD2 can give a user an overall view of their finances. EU businesses could get an overall view of all currency held with Account Servicing PSPs. PSD2 gives the user of a currency account the right to use an AISP. This could allow crowdsourced exchanges on peer-to-peer FX platforms.

There is still a lot of EU trade that triggers a currency exchange. A lot of the currency held by EU businesses are in currency accounts and businesses will have a right to give AISPs access to the information in those accounts. Businesses will also have a right to give PISPs permission to initiate payments from those accounts. The PSD2 APIs seem likely to assist the growth of peer-to-peer FX platforms.

SME Accounting

Accounting software providers for SMEs could use PSD2 APIs. This is a very innovative sector. Cloud-based Accounting Software is replacing older software. The older software was installed at the SME's premises.

Business data is uploaded into the Cloud by the staff of the SME and they can use mobile devices to upload data. Some SMEs don't have a full-time Accountant. The Accountancy firm that prepares the SME's accounts can see this data in the Cloud.

This has many advantages over software installed on the premises. **With Cloud Accounting, the SME's Accountancy firm can see transactions every day and this helps errors to be spotted quickly.** This saves the staff a huge effort at the end of the year and it stops a big effort at the annual tax deadline. The Cloud design also allows receipts to be scanned. Transactions can be recorded by SME staff while they are with customers and invoices can be issued as soon as a job is finished.

SMEs have been using service providers to screen scrape their account data from their banks. The service provider uses security details disclosed by the SME. The service provider enters the SME's online banking service and scrapes out the banking data. This automates the reconciliation of the SME's book keeping with its bank records. Because it is automated, it can take place every day. This can play a big part in producing accurate and fast information on the SME's profits.

This screen scraping process causes the same risks for an SME as it does for consumers. The SMEs have to allow the screen scraping service provider to use sensitive data and private passwords. This gives the service provider the authority to act as the SME. PSD2 will create a legally certain environment for SMEs. An AISP can extract the bank data and can insert bank data into SME weekly and monthly cash flow analysis. SME Management and their Accountancy firms will quickly spot changes in profits.

Fast and clear data is very important if SMEs are trying to borrow money. Many SMEs rely on loans to help them grow. PSD2 could increase the growth of SME Cloud Accounting in the EU and could help growing SMEs to borrow money.

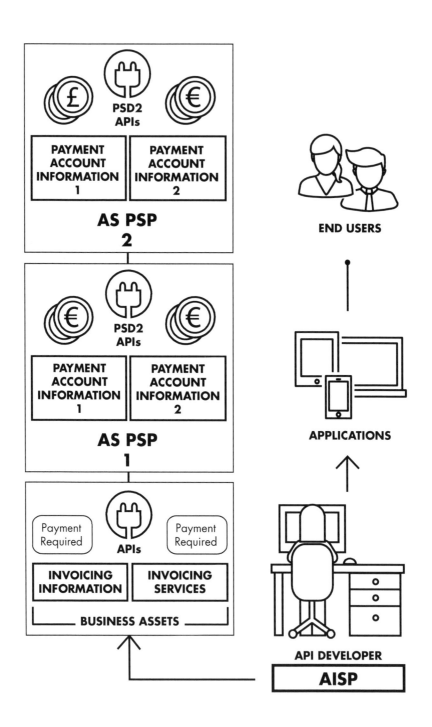

External Audit

External Auditors are interested in the payment accounts used by their clients. Auditors may use payment account data available at PSD2 APIs.

Auditors investigate information that is prepared by somebody else. They investigate claims that a firm makes in its financial statements. The financial statements explain how a firm makes its money and how it spends money. They give information on how much cash a firm has and explain how the firm records information about its assets.

Cash movements in payment accounts often provide direct evidence to Auditors. Sometimes the cash movements don't provide all the evidence needed. They can still be a starting point to investigate other records held by a firm.

Auditors spend time and money to gather evidence and they form an opinion about the accuracy of financial statements. They prepare extensive documents before they meet a client. They interview employees of the client firm and they study how the firm tries to prevent fraud. They choose samples of records to examine and these samples help the Auditor decide if the financial statements are accurate. Perhaps one-third of Auditors activities focus on cash moving through payment accounts.

Businesses get cash by selling goods and services and they record this as revenues. Auditors want to be sure that a firm is not overstating revenues because overstating revenues is a fraud. It makes financial statements appear more attractive to investors. Large amounts of data on business revenues will be available through PSD2 APIs.

Businesses use cash to buy goods and services. Perhaps half a firm's routine activities involve purchasing. An Auditor will check for evidence that the cash outgoings in financial statements match data in payment accounts. Trading firms have a predictable pattern to their purchases and Auditors focus on patterns of purchasing data. They look for unusual purchases and strange patterns. Unusual purchases can mean that money is being diverted.

A firm's Board of Directors needs to understand a firm's cash movements. Potential investors, trade creditors and regulatory agencies all have an interest in payment account data.

Larger firms can have many payment accounts because this can improve a firm's internal controls. They may have a dedicated payment account for wages. This allows staff to handle wages while only having access to certain information. It also limits their access to the firm's cash. An AISP can gather information across all payment accounts in one bank.

Companies might also use the services of more than one bank because this creates more competition between banks. An AISP can gather information from payment accounts in many EU banks.

Audit risks could be reduced if payment account data could be gathered and sampled more effectively. An Auditor can never check every single transaction. PSD2 could allow Auditors to check more transactions and this will reduce risk. More errors and frauds will be spotted. PSD2 could improve auditing in the EU.

Tax Collection

One Government Department has the job of collecting taxes. All other Government Departments spend public money. Taxes fund expenditure by the spending Departments. Expenditure is planned in advance, so it's a problem if taxes are lower than forecast. It's also a problem if taxes are higher than forecast because the spending Departments may have stopped important projects. Governments try to improve the forecasts of tax receipts.

Forecasting future taxes is not easy. Governments raise a lot of taxes based on the number of people at work. They also raise taxes based on money that people spend. An unexpected increase in economic activity causes an unexpected increase in taxes. The same connection exists in an unexpected reduction in economic activity so this causes volatility in the taxes raised. Governments try to avoid unexpected changes in tax receipts.

Governments can borrow money and they often borrow money when spending is higher than tax receipts. A Government can quickly increase or decrease spending. Managing the income from taxes is more difficult. Taxpayers can change their behaviour if tax rates change. Taxpayers can pay their taxes in lumps rather than in regular amounts. There is also uncertainty when tax payers assess their own tax liabilities. Governments try to reduce this uncertainty.

EU Member States manage uncertain tax receipts. The EU aims to ensure that decisions are taken as closely as possible to the citizen. Regular checks are made to confirm that action at EU level is justified. This is called the Subsidiarity principle. The EU also has a principle of Proportionality. Proportionality requires that the EU only does what is necessary to achieve the objectives of EU Treaties. Taxation policy in the EU takes account of Subsidiarity and Proportionality so the EU doesn't have a fully harmonised tax system.

Extra efforts are being made to stop tax evasion.
Many countries have agreed on a "Common Reporting Standard (CRS)" and most EU Member States are in this group. CRS is an agreement to share data on taxpayers' assets and incomes. Before CRS, information was shared on request and sharing information on request was not fully effective in preventing tax evasion. CRS will transfer relevant information automatically and systematically.

CRS will cause a big increase in reporting by banks. Banks will have to disclose details of their account holders and will also identify accounts for reporting as they are opened. Interest, balances and large transactions will have to be reported. Tax authorities in CRS countries will swap reported information once a year. Bank account data is now a keystone of cooperation on tax evasion.

CRS is just one measure to increase tax compliance in the EU. Digitalisation of tax collection is another key measure. The investigation of potential non-compliance is becoming digital. Enforcement is becoming digital and tax authorities are checking data from many sources. This helps them get a full picture of a taxpayer's income and expenditure.

Payment accounts contain data about taxable activities. Income from jobs and pensions flow into payment accounts. Investment income and business revenues also flow into payment accounts. Tax authorities try to understand the links between taxpayers to see certain behaviours and patterns.

Other digital records also interest tax authorities. Digital data comes from publicly owned land registries and vehicle licensing agencies. Other data can come from publicly available sources such as social media and online marketplaces.

Payment accounts are used by tax payers that assess their own tax bills. These tax payers are naturally more interesting for tax authorities. Most EU Member States use some self-assessment in their taxation regimes. Taxpayers that are self-employed are asked to assess their tax bills. People with complex tax affairs or a high income are asked to self-assess their taxes. This usually takes place once a year.

Some tax self-assessment will become an entirely digital process. This will be in the form of a "digital tax account". These digital tax accounts will be like online bank accounts. Probable tax bills will be pre-populated into these digital tax accounts. Interest paid in bank accounts is an expected liability that will be pre-populated.

Tax authorities usually have legal power to obtain bank data on suspected tax evaders. They can also have legal power to directly take unpaid taxes from bank accounts. They can also enter a business premises to examine records.

Tax authorities tend not to use formal legal powers immediately. They find higher risk categories of taxpayer who do not voluntarily self-assess their liabilities. They may review a specific industry that is believed to have a higher non-compliance profile. They may make unannounced site visits.

These interventions are designed to avoid expensive formal audits. They also allow the taxpayer to admit to undeclared taxes. PSD2 APIs will be an efficient way for tax authorities to get bank data. It could be in the taxpayer's interest to give permission for a tax authority to extract bank data. As a formal investigation has not started, tax authorities can treat this disclosure as "unprompted". Tax authorities can allow taxpayers to make an extra payment without facing a legal penalty.

Tax Authorities may consider becoming AISPs. **The availability of payment account data will allow more no-penalty interventions with tax payers.** This higher number of early interventions will save public money. It will help avoid the costs of formal audits where more expensive methods are used.

Tax authorities have a big interest in data mining and they are interested in the API economy. As state agencies, firms and banks publish APIs, tax authorities can gather and cross-check more data. Tax authorities can use their legal powers to get access to this data.

Banks are required to provide a lot of data to public bodies. There could be duplicated effort for banks on CRS and PSD2. CRS and PSD2 requires similar data. Banks need software architecture that minimises these unavoidable costs.

Social Activity

There are a lot of sporting and social clubs in the EU. It is estimated that 200 million of the EU population participate in sport at least once a week. EU banks do not prioritise this market segment but a social media platform that is used across the EU might prioritise this segment.

Social media platforms are interested in social activity. **Social activities cost money and this money has to be managed.** Social media platforms could use the payment account data from the PSD2 APIs to help manage this money.

Banks don't prioritise social and sporting clubs because they buy few financial products. Local clubs and societies do not have big deposits. Clubs typically do not borrow. Clubs buy equipment locally so they don't need foreign exchange. Clubs often do not accept Credit or Debit Cards because they only collect membership fees once a year. Clubs specialise in particular activities so this reduces the number of supplier payments. Club management is often voluntary so this removes a need for a payroll service.

Social activities have both non-financial and financial issues. Social media helps sports and social clubs deal with the non-financial issues. Social media can help a small group coordinate their activities. They organise, agree objectives, discuss issues, post photos and share content.

Voluntary officials struggle with the financial management challenge. A payment account in the name of the club will be required and a bank will usually ask for two officials to agree a movement of funds. A club's treasurer must maintain records of the financial affairs of the club. There must be back-up arrangements to avoid loss of data. Social and sporting clubs have a high turnover of voluntary officials. This causes problems in information management and it slows down decision making on financial issues.

Social and sporting clubs are heavy users of cash, cheques, spreadsheets and receipt books. **People can be frequent users of modern technology in their professional lives and yet be forced to revert to old fashioned methods as volunteer club officials.**

PSD2 could allow Social Media to improve the financial management of social activity. A Social Media platform could act as a PISP and AISP. Financial management services for clubs can be an overlay on top of existing banking arrangements. This would improve competition and it would help develop the EU's digital economy. PSD2 could improve the effectiveness of managing social activity in the EU.

New Business Models for EU Banks

Software Architecture

Banks will have to change their business models for the API Economy. Banks will share data and processes and their internal systems will be exposed. They will need to invest in their software architecture and they must design software that can connect to the API Economy.

There is a relationship between a firm's structure and the design of its products. Products tend to mirror a firm's structure. A firm looks for solutions in a constrained environment. Communication patterns can follow rigid pathways. Firms can have fixed ways of solving problems and this leaves an imprint on how products are designed.

Most established banks are organised in a similar fashion. This influences the evolution of the industry. People designing banking solutions work in one bank and they can often work within one project. They are following one timetable. They are often in the same building and can be in the same room. They adopt a similar behaviour. Organisational design is often imprinted in the design of banking solutions.

Peoples' goals in a tightly organised firm are shared and targets are written down. Deadlines are clear. Software designers in a bank have formal contracts and they respond to a formal authority.

There are other types of organisations that develop software. Software can be developed by "open source" communities. A person owns the rights to an original version of software but that person doesn't try to make profits directly from those rights. The software is made available so that it can be improved by anyone. It can be distributed by anyone and used for any purpose. Open source software is developed in a collaborative and public way. The person who owned the rights to the original version can make a profit indirectly from the success of the software.

The organisation that works on open source software is loose and informal. The programmers have no formal commercial relationship. They are much less tight-knit than the software developers in one firm.

The open source community develops software that is segmented. **It has similar characteristics to a prefabricated building because different sections of software are designed in different places.** Changes made to one section have little impact on the others. Open source projects need to build software in sections as it allows a loose community to work together.

It is different when mature firms like banks design software. The aim of the single team is a product that is fast and has lots of features. They don't aim to build software in sections. This product might have to be changed in the future. It is not built in sections and one change can have a big ripple effect. It can be difficult to keep improving a product with this design. Customers like products to be improved quite often.

Tightly organised banks offer packaged solutions and the packages contain multiple services. A customer could buy all their services in this package but the packages can also have more services than some customers need. There is a lot at stake for customers if the package falls behind on quality or price.

API Developer communities will spring up around the PSD2 APIs. API Developers are not an open source community and they are not working on a single application. However, API Developer communities have loose and informal relationships. **API Developers are not centrally coordinated within a formal organisational structure.** The small and nimble API Developers have narrow commercial aims and simpler organisational structures. Behaviour in a developer community emerges independently. Loosely connected and informal organisations of small providers will cluster together through APIs.

These loosely connected groups of API Developers will innovate at a faster pace than banks. One member of the informal group could have an improved feature every day. This will strengthen the overall position of the loosely connected group.

PSD2 will make banking processes and data available to loosely connected groups of nimble organisations. APIs will allow data in each section of software to be matched. The customer's data will flow between the loosely connected community of developers. If one of the small providers falls behind in quality or price, a replacement can be picked by the customer.

Customers can add new sections from different providers as their needs develop. Loose groups of API Developers will influence the evolution of the EU financial services market after PSD2.

Banks will want to collaborate with API Developers but they will also want to compete with them. One of the ways to compete and collaborate is to have a Service

Oriented Architecture (SOA). SOA helps firms connect services that are managed by software.

With SOA, business services are assembled by a set of "building blocks". The building blocks are available off-the-shelf. If they are not available off-the-shelf, SOA enables them to be built quickly. The architecture defines the building blocks to use and says how they should interact with each other. SOA can help systems development in mature firms to be nimbler.

SOA will help banks in the API economy. Most banks struggle to shield customers from old, well-established systems which approve payments and confirm balances on accounts. The older systems also organise and run timetables for loans and deposits.

Banks have good reasons to shield customers from core systems. These systems have been in place for many years. Some of these systems were installed before the Internet and many were installed before mobile phones. Core banking systems struggle to keep pace with modern business.

Requests to IT departments in banks keep coming. Banks don't want to keep on reinventing the wheel because it is very expensive. Banks want computer programs they can easily reuse and easily maintain. They want it to be easy to share data and resources.

Not all mature industries are the same. Some industries are mature and change very slowly. The cement industry in 50 years' time won't be hugely different from the cement industry 50 years ago. Some mature industries can change dramatically. Media firms are a good example. The arrival of the Internet means that the media industry has had to radically change. New ways of making profits must be found. New products, new partnerships and new customers are needed. Banking is a very mature industry and it must radically change.

Many large businesses have built very complex software code that has accumulated over the past 20 years. Banks are long established businesses and they have been building software applications for many years. Many core systems in banks meet the needs of just one department or solve only one particular problem. As things change, these systems are patched up. They don't easily adapt to a changing environment. Banks don't have systems that can be used for several purposes and they cannot be reused several times.

Some banks have become very large over time and they have become very complex to manage. Banks have organised their people into divisions with different targets for product development and profitability. People want a lot of influence over systems design for their division so they can be slow to share software with other divisions.

Banks have rules that are buried deep in core systems and these rules can be written into the software code of individual applications. Managers can struggle to know if their business strategies are in these rules. These rules run the business on a daily basis. The rules decide what a customer is charged and decide what a salesperson will earn. The rules decide on the discounts that a supplier gets and the revenues to be shared with a partner.

Older systems can struggle to make sure that a bank complies with regulations. Regulators want only certain employees to change critical systems and they want evidence that a business practice always complies with a regulation. Older systems can struggle to tell whether regulations are being met.

Some of the old software applications run unique practices and these unique practices can be at the heart of the business. An online store can accept an order in one keyboard click. A university can allow all its libraries to be searched at the one time. A bank can check account balances and allow payments by its customers.

These practices are often tightly linked into an old software application and they cannot be changed easily. A business could grow if it could make these practices available for partners. This valuable practices could be made available through APIs. **The business world is getting more competitive and banks need ways to sell more of their products and services.**

SOA will make it easier for banks to share data and resources. They can reuse data and resources with more partners. Getting to SOA world is a painstaking journey for a mature firm. It takes planning, time and patience. The journey is more difficult for a large and complex business like a bank.

SOA and APIs are concerned with services that are managed by software. The core concept of SOA is the notion of a service. Services are self-contained. The people who use them don't see the building blocks under the surface. This building block design also applies to APIs. The difference between services and APIs is the intended user. APIs are designed to be attractive to a commercial API Developer. Services within a business are designed with reuse and cost savings in mind.

Some banks will successfully streamline their software architecture. This will help them grow and innovate in the API Economy. Other banks could struggle to develop their software architecture so they will struggle to connect to the API Economy.

Risk Management

Banks will need to manage the risks and rewards of the API Economy. Banks have lots of risk from day to day activities. They have lots of internal processes and procedures need to be up to date. Staff are human and they make mistakes. External events can be unexpected and they can cause unexpected problems with products. APIs are a type of product so APIs will have risks for banks to manage.

Nimble new service providers are quite advanced in API risk management. They have processes that use Public APIs. Their data is opened up to partners and customers through APIs. They don't have legacy technology like banks and their architecture copes with growth and complexity.

Banks are not familiar with the commercial use of APIs so they will have to adapt their risk management. The biggest risk is that the technology that runs the PSD2 APIs has problems. PISPs and AISPs will build services that rely on banks' PSD2 APIs and this is a new challenge for banks. Public APIs can be used by firms who do not have a wider relationship with a bank. The PSD2 APIs are very high profile due to the Regulatory intervention. There is increased reach and increased volume from Public APIs so this increases a bank's overall risk profile.

PSD2 brings compliance risk because banks need to comply with PSD2. There will also be an Industry Rulebook to deal with exceptional situations. The exceptional situations will be disputes, rejects, returns, refusals and refunds relating to APIs. Banks need to follow the Rulebook.

Banks will need to plan capacity for this new activity. They will need to estimate how often the APIs will be used so they can plan for the growth in the service. They will need to plan for the amount of data that the APIs will carry so that any surge in API volumes doesn't cause problems. The internal IT support levels for the APIs will be high. The internal IT support will carry out quality assurance on the APIs so that they deliver the expected results.

PSD2 could make customers more relaxed about disclosing their online banking security details.
This could increase the risk of hacking and fraud.

APIs are like any other input in the business supply chain. Risk managers need to start thinking about the risks of using APIs. Losing access to an API is like losing a key raw material. Businesses that use APIs should identify alternatives and they need to regularly review their rights to use these APIs.

Banks have a risk to their reputations from PSD2. Banks acting as Account Servicing PSPs must treat PISPs and AISPs in a fair way. Banks cannot make them sign a commercial agreement. Banks cannot force PISPs and AISPs to carry out their business in a particular way. They cannot treat them as a low priority or put payments initiated by PISPs at the end of the queue. If there is evidence of fraud or unauthorised access to an account, banks can refuse to take instructions from a PISP or AISP. The PSD2 law says that banks must give reasons if they refuse.

There will be a lot at stake if PSD2 APIs unexpectedly fail. Money is a very sensitive area. The PSD2 APIs will report on peoples' money and move peoples' money. This is more sensitive than using Google Maps. A visitor in a strange city can still find their way if their smartphone loses access to Google Maps. A taxi-driver can phone you to get directions to your house. An API Developer that has a problem with Google Maps API can get another mapping API quickly.

PSD2 APIs will carry out crucial financial tasks. It is a big problem if a family cannot buy food due to a delay in a wage payment. The stakes are high. Wage payments that rely on PSD2 APIs could be disrupted. There can be a long ripple effect from missed wage payments. When wages don't arrive, loan repayments don't get made. Utility bills are missed and routine spending gets delayed.

PSD2 is the law and moving money is a high stakes business. However, a bank will still need plans to switch off access to an API.

Banks are unlikely to switch off PSD2 APIs due to legal issues. The EU law makers have made the legal environment clear. The Account Servicing PSP distributes these services and data under EU law. This is established in the PSD2 framework. Customer permission will be recorded using the Technical Standards. The rights of the businesses that are using the API are set out in the PSD2 framework.

A PISP or AISP could use PSD2 data for more purposes than agreed with the customer. This is a breach of PSD2. The PSD2 rules do refer to fraud or unauthorised access to an account. In these situations, banks can refuse to take instructions from a PISP or AISP. There are structures under PSD2 for making complaints.

If banks decide to add additional APIs to the PSD2 APIs, the risks become more complex.

A bank must open data from a currency account through PSD2 APIs. The bank could also distribute streaming foreign exchange rates as an API. The market data could actually be owned by Reuters or Bloomberg so banks will need a Rights Management policy. This will ensure that it does not distribute data that it does not own. A change in a bank's rights could cause some APIs to be withdrawn.

Banks will have to make decisions on trademark constraints. A bank's privacy policies are also relevant. A change in a Bank's Privacy Policies could cause some APIs to be abruptly unavailable.

Banks could see API misuse by a PISP or AISP and respond slowly. This could weaken their legal position. This could be considered "implied consent." In that case, an API could be abruptly withdrawn.

A PISP without access to a PSD2 API has poor choices.
The PISP could try to find a substitute API with similar capabilities. It takes time for a customer to switch to a payment account to another Account Servicing PSP. This is not a realistic contingency plan. The reality is that the PISP would close the payment initiation service. Revenues would halt at the PISP. A bank acting as an Account Servicing PSP needs to manage its reputation. It will need to communicate actively in these situations.

Risk managers in banks need to understand the risk of providing APIs. Banks will also start to become API Developers. More data will flow between different firms. More firms will have services that depend on APIs. If things go wrong, there will be a ripple effect. Risk managers need to understand the likely ripple effects from APIs.

New Skills

Banks will need new skills for the API Economy.
APIs are quite different to the distribution strategies
that banks normally use.

Banks have traditionally had a "hub and spoke" business model. The hub contains huge vaults of customer data.
The hub also contains systems for handling core products.
The core products are payments, accounts, loans and
deposits.

The spokes of the wheel are distribution channels.
These channels carry the bank's brand. The distribution
channels are usually branches, call centres, ATMs,
websites, kiosks, mobile phones, tablets and customer
relationship managers.

The hub and spoke branded model is very established.
Banks have had branches carrying their brands for
many decades. In some cases, bank brands are
hundreds of years old. Call Centres and ATMs have
been around for roughly 30 years, with banking websites
appearing 20 years ago. Kiosks then arrived about 15
years ago while mobile phones saw their first financial
services roughly 5 years later. Tablet banking has been
in place since about 2011.

A bank's customer service has become more modern.
However, the channel management decisions have not
changed. Banks decide which branded channels should
deliver a service. The service is aimed a group
of customers.

PSD2 will make channel decisions more complex. **APIs will be "indirect channels" to market for a bank.** The Developers that use these APIs will be commercially independent. The API Developers' services will physically depend on PSD2 APIs. These Developer services will carry a bank's data but they will not carry the bank's brand.

API Developers will use the PSD2 APIs to experiment. They may experiment far more than a bank's own IT department. The Developers will expect the APIs to allow faster delivery of new services. The APIs should not be difficult to learn.

Banks will have to learn new ways of managing their business. The Developers will want it to be simple to register to use the APIs and expect self-service registration. They will also want an easy way to search for the APIs they need. The APIs need to be sturdy and perform at a predictable speed. This will be particularly important as bank data will be used in important tasks. Banks may need to publish statistics about their APIs to attract Developers.

Banks will have to put together a team to manage APIs. The most logical positioning is a bank's products unit. Within an API Products team, individual Product Managers will carry out the typical Product Manager tasks. They will create an overall Product Roadmap. They will make decisions on product features and improvements. They will monitor how APIs are performing for both Developers and Users. An API has similar characteristics to a product delivered through branded channels.

The API Products team will need strong leadership. The leadership will need to maintain the ongoing support of a bank's most senior staff. The API Products team will need to work particularly well with the own-brand products team. The own-brand products team will be nervous about new competitors accessing data through APIs.

The API Products team needs the right skills for the API Economy. The API Products leadership will need to engage directly with the API Developer community. The API Products leadership must fully understand what APIs can do. The team will need excellent knowledge of EU regulations. They will also need to understand industry rule books that are built for those regulations. The API Products leadership should not be reliant on the bank's compliance department to track proposed EU regulations.

The EU regulatory initiatives are likely to continue and evolve. There will be long consultations with industry participants before new legislation is introduced. Banks with good API strategies will monitor the regulations.

The software engineers that design and maintain the APIs may not be in the management structure of the API Products team. This team could be located within IT. The IT department will already have agreed service levels with the wider Products division of the bank. However, these service levels will be designed for the bank's own brand product range. The internal service level agreements and response times between API Products and IT will need to be considered very carefully.

Flaws in PSD2 APIs will result in bad feedback from Developers. That feedback might go to Regulators. This will cause damage to a bank's reputation.

A Developer Community Manager will be an important role and will need to be a technical person. The Community Manager will actively engage with influential API developers.

New Revenue Streams

PSD2 has reduced the earning power of banks acting as Account Servicing PSPs. They have to offer valuable data and processes without commercial contracts. Banks need new revenue streams to offset this change. Banks have to invest in API management to comply with PSD2 so the API Economy is a logical place to look for new revenue streams.

Banks will make choices about the legal roles they play under PSD2. A traditional bank will be an Account Servicing PSP. A PSP also has an opportunity to act as a PISP, AISP or both. Banks may initiate payments from payments accounts at other banks and may get data from payment accounts at other banks.

Changes to banks' market share from PSD2 could be slow at first. Changes to sales of higher value products could happen faster. The general knowledge in the payment account will be shared with other providers if the customer wishes. PISPs and AISPs will start to build relationships with customers.

Sales of more profitable financial products by the Account Servicing PSP could be damaged by PSD2. The entire business of a new provider could be focused on a single financial product. This will help a new provider to gain a price or quality advantage over the Account Servicing PSP.

Sales of more profitable products by the Account Servicing PSP could also be improved by PSD2. PSD2 will compel banks to participate in the API Economy. Banks could find data or functions in APIs developed by other firms. There could be new information about potential customers from APIs. Sales of some products could be improved if banks and non-banks share data and processes through APIs.

PSD2 will reduce some of the advantages of being an Account Servicing PSP. Banks may see PSD2 APIs as the free part of a "freemium" business model for API Developers. In recent years, freemium has become a popular business model. "Freemium" is a combination of "free" and "premium". Users get basic features at no cost and can choose richer functions for an extra fee.

PSD2 sets out the services that Account Servicing PSPs must offer PISPs and AISPs without a commercial contract. Free data and free processes are powerful marketing tools. Banks acting as Account Servicing PSPs will attract PISPs and AISPs. Banks will want to make gains in the API economy so they will want PISPs and AISPs to choose richer API functions for a fee.

Some APIs will help a bank's direct competitors.
If these are Premium APIs, banks need to earn suitable fees. Some APIs will help both complementary and competing services.

Freemium business models have natural challenges. A bank has a problem if it has PSD2 APIs but offers no premium APIs. A bank has a problem if few API Developers upgrade from PSD2 APIs to Premium APIs. API Developers may not understand the benefits of premium APIs.

A bank will need a target for converting API Developers from PSD2 to Premium APIs. A very low conversion rate to Premium APIs is not good. A very high conversion rate isn't necessarily good either. A very high conversion rate might mean low use of a bank's PSD2 APIs and Premium APIs. A vibrant API Developer community could drive the growth of a rival bank.

Early adopters of Premium APIs will be less price-sensitive than API Developers who come later. **The early arrivals will be API Developers who find Bank APIs very useful.** Conversion rates are likely to dip over time. This will happen when the community expands to include Developers who see less value in Bank APIs.

Banks will see some value from the "Free" API Developers. They may draw in other Developers who use Premium APIs. Significant value could flow from referrals.

A Freemium model commits an API Provider to ongoing innovation. Users who join late will be harder to convert to Premium APIs. Account Servicing PSPs have to keep increasing the value of the Premium APIs. Freemium is both a revenue model and a commitment to innovation.

Customer Segments

EU banks need to have Premium APIs as well as PSD2 APIs. They need to decide the customer segments to target with Premium APIs. Banks will take a different view of Consumer segments and SME segments. They will be focused on segments in their EU regions.

Banks will be concerned that PSD2 will damage sales to Consumers. The activities of a consumer are less complex than a business. Consumer markets can be served with "big data" sales strategies. The potential for a sale of a financial product to a consumer is often signalled by one payment. It is a wage payment into a payment account. The ability of a consumer to borrow can often be checked at a credit reference agency. A credit reference agency collects information on the credit rating of individuals. They make this information available to banks and finance firms.

Banks may be less concerned about PSD2 damaging sales to SMEs. Banks' sales of financial products to SMEs could benefit from APIs. SMEs are more complex customers than Consumers. "Big data" strategies are far more difficult to design for SMEs.

SMEs have payments that are complex and move in many directions. They can have many payment accounts. Unlike Consumers, SMEs can make sales by giving credit to customers and make purchases using credit from suppliers. This data is recorded outside the payment account. This information is very valuable for a bank wishing to offer loans to SMEs. Selling loans to SMEs could be improved if banks and non-banks share data and processes through APIs.

The best examples of the emerging API economy have come from Silicon Valley. Google, Amazon and Facebook have good examples. They have huge numbers of customers across the world and they have achieved success through waves of growth in all markets. Their ambitions are global.

EU banks impacted by PSD2 will take a regional view at first. They will be focused on APIs for customer segments in their home regions. Financial services in the EU is regional in nature and many EU banks are traditional "National Champion" banks. They work closely with providers of digital services in their home markets.

EU banks are not social media platforms aiming for billions of users. The functions that EU banks could bring to the API Economy are powerful. However, their data is heavily regionalised because the valuable data stored in banks is customers' data. Trade between customers follows long established patterns. These regional factors have endured a long time and they will remain influential.

The EU offers two key influences on trade between countries. There is a common regional trading community for 28 countries. There is a common currency for 19 eurozone countries. However, there is also a lot of diversity in the EU. The European Union has 24 official languages. It is the same distance by road between Lisbon and Helsinki as between Los Angeles and New York. There are eight land borders and a ferry crossing between Lisbon and Helsinki.

There are many cultural and geographic influences on trade and investment. There are certain influences that boost trade between two countries. A common language, common colonial history and a common land border influence trade flows. We can call these "home biases". These home biases influence all businesses in a country, not just the banks in a country.

There are some good examples of these home biases. The EU introduced a common currency in 1999 and Spain became a member. However, nearly half of overseas investment by Spanish firms continued to be in Latin America. Europe's larger and closer economy was in second place. These trading patterns continue to this day.

The data contained in payment accounts reflect customers' activities. These customer activities have home biases and the resulting data will have home biases. This will influence the value that PSD2 APIs create.

EU banks gather vast amounts of customer data in their regions and they dominate the recruitment of youthful customers. Banks also lead the process of scrutinising payment flows in their regions. Banks check for money launderers and other corrupt activities. They get a profile of the customer when the payment account is first opened. They keep checking for corrupt activity as the account is being used.

EU banks have strong positions in their home regions and they will focus on the APIs emerging in these regions. Banks will start to extend their market research and they will survey their customers' plans to use APIs.

Key Partnerships

Banks will develop Premium APIs. These Premium APIs could be published as Public APIs and they could also be offered to Partners. Partner APIs are not compelled by PSD2. Banks could use Partner APIs to find new revenue if they offer these APIs on a commercial basis.

Partner APIs could be a "soft launch" for banks' use of APIs. Partner APIs are used to integrate software between a firm and chosen business partners. They are supported by specific contracts and they can also have specific risk management. Dispute management can be planned in detail. Partner APIs could be an interim step for banks on the journey to Public APIs enforced by PSD2.

Partner APIs can be focused on familiar regional markets and they can formally plan the sharing of revenues, assets and data. Staff have to make a business case and Partner APIs have specific aims and fixed timetables. These are familiar innovation management processes in a bank.

Timetable

PSD2 is EU law. It will become law at Member State level in January 2018. Technical Standards won't be ready until September 2018 at the earliest and setting Technical Standards will be a difficult process. It could drag on into early 2019.

Some EU banks could approach PSD2 purely as a compliance project. They will not accelerate investment in Service Oriented Architecture. Actively providing and using APIs will not be in risk management frameworks. They will approach PSD2 as a "Big Bang" event in 2018 or 2019. Product managers will not be trained on APIs.

The final PSD2 Technical Standards will be seen by these banks as a "start line". There won't be any Premium APIs to build new revenues. Nothing will be launched before the final PSD2 deadlines. These banks could let a regional rival become the Partner Bank of choice for local API Developers. These banks could miss a wave of growth and innovation in the API Economy.

Some EU banks will recognise the global move to an API Economy. They won't approach PSD2 as a compliance project. They will accelerate investment in Service Oriented Architecture. Actively providing and using APIs will be built into risk management. They won't approach PSD2 as a "Big Bang" event in 2018 or 2019. Product managers will be trained on APIs

The final PSD2 Technical Standards will be seen by these banks as a "finish line". There will be Premium APIs to build new revenues. Some APIs will go to market before the PSD2 deadlines. These banks will be the Partner Bank of choice for regional API Developers.

PSD2 will help catapult these banks into the heart of the API Economy. These banks could ride a wave of growth and innovation in the API Economy.

INDUSTRY WIDE DEADLINES		
Date	*Legal Impact of PSD2*	*Technical Standards on Security & Strong Authentication*
Jan 2016	**Entry into force at EU level**	
Q2 2016		EBA publish draft standards
Jan 2017		Earliest date for EU to adopt standards
Jan 2018	PSD2 becomes law in EU Member States	
Sep 2018		Earliest date to come into force
Q1 2019		Likely date to come into force

FREEMIUM API STRATEGY		
PSD2 APIs	*Premium Payments APIs*	*Other Premium APIs*

1. Invest in Service Oriented Architecture

2. Develop Risk Management

3. Add API Skills

4. Identify Customer Segments

5. Develop Premium APIs

6. Find Regional Partners

API Developer Community using PSD2 and Premium APIs

8242036R00052

Printed in Germany
by Amazon Distribution
GmbH, Leipzig